Testimo

"This is a book that I feel every leader should read. I wish that I would have known some of the traits of Jezebel operating in our church years ago. I have learned things about the Jezebel spirit that I have not been aware of before. This is a must-read book and I thank Marie Moyer for allowing God to use her through the writing of this book."

~Terri Wilson, Worship Leader, Light of the World Ministries, Marshall Texas, USA~

"Marie and I have stayed in touch for 42 years talking about life and our love of God. Marie is open and honest and has been for as long as I remember, wanting to hear what people had to say."

"Both Marie and I have spent many hours over the years sitting with the Word of God open, searching out the mysteries of God and learning who we are in Him and the truth of His Word. The journey will go on because the Word of God is deeper than the deepest oceans."

"She is a lover of God and His Word and this book is just the start of what He is going to reveal to her and have her faithfully release to the body of Christ. This book is just a small sample of what God has shared with her. Through the teachings of this book I have gained a great wealth of knowledge to help in my prayer life and in how I view Jezebel and the way she works in our lives, seeking to kill and destroy."

"Marie, let God that lives in you shine and illuminate the path he's taking you on."

~Jan Brink, Sister in Christ, Canada~

"The Lord so divinely chose to give us these lessons and Scriptures on the woman Jezebel. Also, in these pages is a stern warning by revelation that any who tolerate this type of woman who calls herself a prophetess and follow her will have to go through intense suffering."

"It should be of every believer's utmost prayerful cries that the Lord will give us strength and wisdom to not tolerate this woman and her impurities. Lord Jesus, deliver us from all evil and all impurities."

"Let us stand strong to know the Lord and His Spirit and cleave to what is good. Jesus, lead us with Your wisdom and power away from all deceit and false teaching. In Jesus' name we have the victory over all false prophets! Amen. Believers, seek the Lord, do good and don't grow weary."

"What the Lord personally showed me through this book is how He was very merciful in giving Jezebel time to repent, but she was unwilling. However, believers can seek the Lord's face in repentance. Our God is merciful, and His mercy endures forever. Lord God, forgive me this sin of tolerating Jezebel and lead me in the right paths. Thank You Jesus, for your sacrifice!"

~Erika Schaffer, Author, Canada~

"Marie's book is a leaders' key. . . A must-have for everyone in leadership. You'll see Jezebel in previously unrevealed ways and learn what it takes to 'get victory' and maintain healthy leadership for the Glory of God"

~Sarah Fisher, Pastor, Zürich, Switzerland~

"I found this book intriguing with its wealth of largely unknown, untapped information. I gave myself to self-reflection as I was reading, as I'm sure everyone else will do. The spirit of Jezebel has influenced everyone's life at some point. This knowledge will help you with self, family and prosperity. I would encourage all to read. Overall, the book is a growing point for spiritual freedom and spiritual maturity. This book is full of informative wisdom."

~Tab Swaney - Disciple of Christ, Arkansas USA~

"Marie's book is amazing. It is a book for the leadership and the congregation. It contains unrevealed information about Jezebel's past that will help you know what direction to pray. You will learn how to get victory and maintain it, glory to God!"

~Teresa Castello, Oklahoma, USA~

"After reading this book tonight my heart is still fluttering. I have experienced this several times around me! Marie, has sure done her studying on this subject above and beyond. This book was eye opening, clear, strong, easy to read, astonishing, detailed and helpful! It has arrived in my life in perfect timing. Thank you, Thank you.

~Kathy Girouard, Louisiana, America~

"I could not put the book down. I found myself wanting to learn more about the topic of Jezebel. To put some perspective on it, I am not a member of a church and do not read scripture, so the topic was very new to me and very intriguing, and in some ways a little of a history lesson. Although I could not totally relate to the scenarios, I do imagine we all come into situations with people who do possess the qualities of the Jezebel. I feel the book enlightened me to be aware of their presence, how to identify them and how to deal with them if I do encounter them."

~Dan G.~

Jezebel Exposed

Marie Moyers

Dedication

I dedicate this book to the Holy Spirit. Holy Spirit. You are my absolute essence and the very core of me. My soul needs you. Your' deep calls out to my deep. My heart longs only after you. I am in awe of you.

~~ Marie ~~

I also dedicate this book to my parents, with very much love and respect. I could never have chosen better parents than those My God chose for me. Dad, God's got this.

~~~ Thank you, Lord ~~~

Special Dedication

I give a very special thanks to my husband, Buf, without your love, faith in God, incredible patience with me, and spiritual contributions, this book would be missing key components that God showed you. Your belief in what God was doing through me is tenacious and sustaining. I love you.

Thank you to all those important prayer warriors who stayed on the wall and prayed for this book to be pulled together and for the enemy to be held back. Your' service to the kingdom will be forever remembered by the Lord of Lord the King of Kings.

Prayer

Dear Lord,

I personally invite You to join me as I read this book. Holy Spirit, lead me and teach me as only You can do. Please anoint me to learn your truth. Help me take my eyes off my own circumstances and to focus entirely on you.

I offer you my love and attention. I offer you my humble respect and reverence. You are my Holy God. Only you alone are worthy of love. Teach me to love You more deeply and to worship You both in spirit and truth. Teach me how to understand and live out all that is written in the volume of the book about me.

In Jesus Mighty Name,
Amen.

Contents

INTRODUCTION:

The Bully Connection

Bullies are a very real part of the world we live in today. They are found everywhere you look, in school, work and church. In this book, I will show you how all the characteristics of Jezebel are displayed in the bully. There is the bully's bully who generally reaches the top of the corporate ladder and is riddled with issues. Their issues have issues. They are narcissistic, and in many cases psychopathic also.

As the Body of Christ, we need to understand who Jezebel is and how she works, trying to destroy our relationships – with family members and friends and with God. There have been times when Jezebel's actions have been going on under our noses and we did not see it because it slithered in undetected.

It is unfortunate whenever the church world refuses to acknowledge demon activity. We are never to give glory to the devil, but we must expose him and become educated in what the Scriptures teach about him and the spirit of Jezebel. The Apostle Paul declared, "we are not ignorant of Satan's devices" (II Corinthians 2:11).

I pray that after you study this book, that should you come across a Jezebel spirit, you will be able to identify it quickly for what it is. This book is designed to enable you to detect and discern when and where a Jezebel spirit is operating and to empower you to have victory over this spirit. We have no need to fear Jezebel or any other evil spirit, for we have authority and power over them through the name of Jesus, the blood of Jesus, and the Word of God.

I suggest you get a buddy, maybe someone else whose life is affected by this spirit, to pair up with you and make this journey together.

CHAPTER 1:

Who is Jezebel?
Basic Characteristics

Jesus described a Jezebel-type person in Revelation chapter two. Around A. D. 95, Jesus said to the church in Thyatira:

"I know your works, love, service, faith, your patience and as for your works, the last are more than the first. Nevertheless, I have a few things against you, because you allow that woman Jezebel, who calls herself a prophetess, to teach and seduce My servants to commit sexual immorality and to eat things sacrificed to idols. And I gave her time to repent of her sexual immorality and she did not repent. Indeed, I will cast her into a sickbed, and those who commit adultery with her into great tribulation, unless they repent of their deeds. I will kill her children with death, and all the churches shall know that I am He that searches the minds and hearts. And I will give to each one of you according to your works" (Revelation 2:19-23, NKJV).

From this passage we can draw several things. First of all, although Jezebel was being allowed to teach in this church, she was not the main leader of the church. From what Jesus said at the first of this address, we know that the main leaders of the church were leading the congregation in love, faith, patience and abundant good works. They were doing good in all those areas except one, tolerating Jezebel. But the trouble was that the leaders were allowing Jezebel to teach in the church.

In her teaching, Jezebel had assumed the role of a leader. Three leading characteristics that we immediately see from Jesus' description of this Jezebel are: (1) she placed herself in the role of a leader/teacher in the church, (2) she was sexually immoral and she led others into immorality, and (3) she claimed to be a prophetess, or to operate in prophetic gifts. However, when one lives a life of sexual immorality and still attempts to "press in" and prophesy and operate as a prophet, a spirit of witchcraft will give this person counterfeit gifts.

Jezebel was a false prophetess. We should remember what Jesus taught about false prophets: *"Beware of false prophets, who come to you in sheep's clothing, but inwardly they are ravenous wolves. You will know them by their fruits. Do men gather grapes from thorn bushes or figs from thistles? Even so, every good tree bears good fruit, but a bad tree bears bad fruit. A good tree cannot bear bad fruit, nor can a bad tree bear good fruit. Every tree that does not bear good fruit is cut down and thrown into the fire.* **Therefore by their fruits you will know them***"* (Matthew 7:15-20, NKJV).

Jesus **didn't** say, "By their gifts you will know whether they are true or false". He said, "by their **fruit** you will discern who they are". If the fruit of their ministry is leading people away from God and into sin, they are false.

When Jesus named this person in the church "Jezebel", He was saying that this person was yielding to the same evil spirits as did the Jezebel in the Old Testament. General Jehu, who knew Jezebel well, asked Jezebel's son Joram, *"What peace, as long as the harlotries of your mother Jezebel and her witchcraft are so many?"* (II Kings 9:22)

Jezebel loved the worship of Baal, which included sexual immorality. Baal worship employed numbers of male and female prostitutes. Just like the Jezebel who was teaching at the church of Thyatira, the Old Testament Jezebel was a leader among God's people who promoted sexual immorality.

The Jezebel of the Old Testament also practiced witchcraft and she hated the word of God so much that she tried to kill all the true prophets of the Lord (I Kings 18:4). Jezebel has no respect for authority, and she is dead-set against the will of God. She has the attitude that:

"Nothing is too precious

and no price is too great for me."

She is determined not to let anything stand in the way of her accomplishing her agenda.

If you confront someone who has a Jezebel spirit about their behavior, their reaction is liable to be mean and hateful. They will judge you, condemn you, and put you down. If you have a dream or vision which reveals the sin of a Jezebel and you tell it to them, don't expect them to receive it. Jezebel hates the word of the Lord. She will immediately have "a revelation from the Spirit" that you are wrong. The implication is always, "You've got a problem; I don't."

Sad to say, there are "Jezebels" in the world today. Who are they? A Jezebel can be a man or a woman, but is a false leader or one attempting to become a leader, who has an evil power behind him or her.

He or she is yielded to evil spirits who function in the ways of sexual immorality and witchcraft. Also, one led by a Jezebel spirit "hates" the word of the Lord with a passion. When dealing with a Jezebel, we do well to heed:

"Put on the whole armor of God, that you may be able to stand against the schemes of the devil. For we do not wrestle against flesh and blood, but against the rulers, against the authorities, against the cosmic powers over this present darkness, against the spiritual forces of evil in the heavenly places" (Ephesians 6:11-12, ESV).

Such evil powers are sent out by Satan and they come to work out his destructive plans (Isaiah 14:3-21, Revelation 2:24).

CHAPTER 2:

Where it All Started: the Jezebel of Elijah's Day

In order to understand who Jezebel is today, we are going to look at who she was in the Bible. Pay close attention to her characteristics. I want you to see the connection to those traits in the bullies in your life today.

In 931 B.C. the original nation of Israel was torn into two nations, Israel to the north and Judah to the south. By then, Israel was completely tormented by internal tribal differences creating openings to frequent invasions. Still, most people there solidly followed the belief that Yahweh was the "one and only true" God.

Phoenicia was located to Israel's north, and as a whole, was cosmopolitan, populous and religiously diverse. Near the beginning of the 9th century B.C., a Phoenician princess named Jezebel was born, the daughter of King Ethbaal. Ethbaal was the King of Sidon, the land which today it is called Lebanon.

Ethbaal was a High Priest of Asherah. At birth, Jezebel was dedicated to the god Baal, and she grew up with her heart completely turned to that god as well as other gods.

Jezebel is not even her birth name.

Her Phoenician name was **Abizebel,** meaning, *"My Father (Baal) is Noble."* The Hebrew scribes deliberately dropped a letter from her name. Therefore, she would be known forever as Jezebel, a dishonorable name meaning, *"Lacking Honor".*

(Brown-Driver-Briggs Hebrew and English Lexicon, Unabridged, Electronic Database. 2002, 2003, 2006 Jezebel Proper name. Also See the Nelson Study Bible, footnote at I Kings 17)

For the purpose of this book we will refer to her as Jezebel.

She was a Phoenician princess who later became the wife of King Ahab of Israel. In the centuries since her death, she has acquired numerous references in popular culture, none of them flattering. Like the account of Cleopatra, Jezebel's story is one of romance and ultimately, the fall of an entire nation.

Jezebel's name has been used for thousands of years to describe a ruthless, proud, and vicious woman. Her name has also become associated with idolaters, prostitutes and witches. This agrees with the two major traits of a Jezebel, which as Jesus pointed out, are sexual immorality and false prophesying (Revelation 2:20-21).

The Bible does not describe Jezebel's childhood, but from deductive reasoning, it is assumed that she lived in a fine home and was educated by the best tutors. Her family worshipped many gods, the most important being Baal, a nature god. King Ethbaal solved his problems by killing anyone who opposed him. It is suggested that this is where Jezebel learned her behavior.

While Jezebel was growing up, Israel crowned a new king, Ahab, the son of Omri. He became king of Israel in the thirty-eighth year of Asa King of Judah (I Kings 16:30).

Ahab ruled from Samaria and, *"did even more open evil before God than anyone yet - a new champion in evil! It wasn't enough for him to copy the sins of Jeroboam son of Nebat; no, he went all out, first by marrying Jezebel daughter of Ethbaal king of the Sidonians, and then by serving and worshiping the god Baal.*

He built a temple for Baal in Samaria, and then furnished it with an altar for Baal. Worse, he went on and built a shrine to the sacred whore Asherah. He made the God of Israel angrier than all the previous kings of Israel put together" (I Kings 16:30-33, The Message).

"It was under Ahab's rule that Hiel of Bethel refortified Jericho, but at a terrible cost. He ritually sacrificed his first born son Abiram at the laying of the foundation, and his youngest son Segub at the setting up of the gates. This is exactly what Joshua son of Nun said would happen" (I Kings 16:34, The Message; also see Joshua 6:26).

To create an alliance with Israel, King Omri arranged for his son, Ahab, to marry Jezebel. How or where the strong-minded idolatrous woman and the king met, we are not told.

Their marriage cemented a political alliance. It was meant to be a peace treaty, but it became a costly compromise for the people of God. The marriage required that Israel follow the political practices of Ahab's new life.

Jezebel was a gifted woman, but she would prostitute all her gifts for the further advancement of evil, and her misdirected talents became a curse. She was persuasive, but her influence was wrongly directed.

As Queen of Israel, she used her strength of will to destroy a king and to pollute the life of a nation. Sounds like a bully's bully.

Contrary to popular belief, Jezebel herself was never a prostitute, but she encouraged this behavior in others by setting up just right environment and carefully placing the idols of Baal in the temple of God.

As a Jew, Ahab sinned against God and his Hebrew faith in taking as his wife the daughter of a man whose very name, Ethbaal, meant, "A Man of Baal." God had forbidden the Jews to marry people from other nations.

But even worse than the sin of marrying a heathen was the fact that Jezebel was a <u>priestess of Baal</u>, a worshiper of idols, and that she had no intention of forsaking those idols and serving the One and only God, the God of Abraham, Isaac and Jacob.

Remember her legal birth name was Abizebel and it means "My father Baal is Noble."

Jezebel would not be able to operate without an Ahab, who gave her status as a queen. A person with a Jezebel spirit needs those in authority to give him or her credibility and respect as a minister.

If no one in Thyatira would have gone to the false prophetess Jezebel's meetings, or received her ministry in any way, she would have been so powerless that she might have moved to another place, looking for followers.

Once Jezebel was married to Ahab, she gained more authority, since she now was the queen of Israel. But did she respect the God-given authority of her husband? No!

She made him a slave to her will and influenced him to worship idols. She was also determined to destroy the worship of Jehovah. Both Ahab and Jezebel lived lives consisting of the very things God hates.

Ahab promoted and participated in Baal and Astarte worship. He allowed sexual rites—homosexuality, bestiality, men and women prostitutes and every disgraceful perversion.

Ahab is also known for his doublemindedness. He was often found waffling between righteousness and the ungodly ways of his wife, Jezebel. As part of the marriage agreement in the alliance between the two kingdoms, he completely incorporated her foreign gods and religious practices into Israel's culture.

This is one of the reasons God commanded Israel not to take any wives from among the conquered people. They did not have a covenant with God and would not be able to understand Gods ways.

Jezebel was stubborn, self-willed, selfish, confrontational, controlling, possessive, and full of hatred, resentment, bitterness, witchcraft and idolatry. All of these traits are in bullies today.

She also had a murderous spirit. She was determined that nothing would stop her from getting what she wanted, and she was manipulative and controlling.

I Kings 21:1-16 clearly reveals how the couple – one with an inward personality and the other with an outward personality - linked together to form a union to accomplish wicked things.

Jezebel was domineering, manipulative and seductive. She intimidated, threatened, lied and did whatever it took to accomplish her end. She had a rebellious spirit and rebellion is witchcraft (I Samuel 15:23).

Since Jezebel flowed in witchcraft, one with a Jezebel spirit has supernatural help in knowing and sensing information. The Delilah spirit gathers information (Judges 16). If she uses this against you, she may say, "I can't tell you how I know this, except I just know it by the spirit".

This is not the Holy Spirit, but the help of a clairvoyant or familiar spirit. Clairvoyance may be defined as the power to perceive things that are out of the range of human senses.

King Ahab could be a weak, withdrawn, and fearful man who tolerated wickedness. He showed himself to be a coward when he agreed to give Ben-Hadad, king of Syria, all of his silver and gold and his wives and children if the Syrian king would leave him alone and not attack him (I Kings 20:1-4).

However, after Ahab was encouraged by a prophet of God, he led his small, outnumbered army against Ben-Hadad and his great multitude of 32 kings with their forces. With God's help, Ahab defeated Ben-Hadad in two successive battles (I Kings 20:5-34).

Ahab conquered more land for Israel than any king except Solomon. He was a mighty warrior, but he was still controlled by Jezebel. He would not stand up for righteousness.

His spirit was so passive that he allowed Jezebel to bring in the nature and fertility god, Baal.

Many people of Israel, and the Yahweh prophet Elijah, despised her actions. Her citizens' displeasure came to a critical point when she brought 800 Baal prophets into Israel and ordered the murder of as many Yahweh prophets as she could find (I Kings 18:4).

At this pivotal moment, Elijah, the leading Jewish prophet of the day appeared. Elijah then gave a prophecy that a terrible drought would come upon Israel. Soon famine and drought spread across Jezebel's land. This sent Jezebel into a flying rage.

Several years later, Ahab died in a battle against the Syrians, and the general named Jehu was promised a crown if he killed Jezebel's son Joram. It is thought that Joram would have rule just as his mother did, in the same dictatorship style.

General Jehu quickly killed Joram, and then made his way to Jezebel's palace to murder her. She, expecting him, applied makeup and dressed herself in her best. Her actions have been interpreted in a variety of ways. Some people believe she was simply dressing for a dignified death.

Others believe she painted herself in hopes of seducing Jehu and becoming his mistress. This is my belief, because one of the main traits of Jezebel is manipulation. Also, she was filled with pride, so she was confident that all would be well with her. By her actions she could have been saying, "Can't you see I am too beautiful to murder?"

In the end, her very own eunuchs threw her out of her upper floor bedroom window onto the ground at Jehu's request. Then she was trampled by Jehu's chariot horses and eaten by dogs, just as Elijah had prophesied. As it will come to be the overthrowing of the Jezebel spirit will be done by the body of christ at the order and timing of the Lord Almighty.

I want to note here that a parent with these strong traits will raise up one or more children who will exhibit the same traits, and through the bloodline they will carry on where the parent left off.

The Jezebel of the Old Testament was influenced by the idol gods that she worshipped. These idol powers are demonic spirits who move in to deceive humanity.
(I Corinthians 10:19-20).

For us to be victorious over the Jezebel spirit, we need to first discern the spirits who are behind Jezebel, the person. Then the key to victory over the spirits is to *not tolerate them.*

No one who operates *in a Jezebel spirit* is going to have any lasting power over the church unless we tolerate her and allow her to have a place of "ministry" (Revelation 2:20).

CHAPTER 3:

For Prayer Warriors and Deliverance Ministers

Sometimes the Bible tells us a specific name of an evil spirit, such as *"Mammon,"* who is the god or evil spirit of greed (Matthew 6:24, Luke 16:9, 11, 13). Another example is *"Molech,"* a Canaanite god (evil spirit) to whom they sacrificed babies (Leviticus 18:21, 20:2-5, 2 Kings 23:10, Jeremiah 32:35). Today, this is still being done through abortion and in some demonic cults.

When the Bible tells us the name of a specific spirit, we should become familiar with that name from the Bible and use it. Just as it is more powerful to pray specific prayers than to pray general prayers, it is sometimes more powerful to use the Bible name for the exact spirit we are casting out, rather than just to call them "demons" or "unclean spirits".

There Must Be a Willing Heart and Soul and Real Repentance

If we are certain that what we are dealing with is a Jezebel spirit in a person, we can bind and cast it out **if** the person is willing to fully repent. You can ask them, "Do you want to be free from this spirit, now and for the rest of your life?" Jesus said that Jezebel (a person with a Jezebel spirit) must repent (Revelation 2:20-23).

The person must hunger and thirst for righteousness and hate the sins to which he or she has been enslaved. Just as Jesus cursed the fig tree at the root, we must first deal with the root of the problem in order to have full and lasting success. What is the root problem in the case of one with the Jezebel spirit? The root of the problem is **in the person** who needs to be delivered.

The Person with a Jezebel Spirit Must Humble Themselves.

First of all, to get to the root of the problem and bring deliverance, we must realize that humbling oneself is the step which comes before repentance (II Chronicles 7:14). Those with a Jezebel spirit have a spirit of pride.

By calling herself a prophetess, Jezebel was thinking more highly of herself than she should (Revelation 2:20). The proud and haughty spirit is referred to again and again in the book of Proverbs: *"Proud and haughty scorner is his name, who deals in proud wrath"* (Pr. 21:24, KJV). Notice the name of this evil spirit is "scorner," or "scoffer". It is mentioned several times in the book of Proverbs (3:34, 16:18, 22:10, 9:7-8, 13:1, 14:16, 24:9, 29:8).

A "scorner" is an individual who is dominated by a spirit of scorn. Their thinking is so influenced by the spirit that they take on the same personality as that spirit: *"He who corrects a scoffer gets shame for himself, and he who rebukes a wicked man only harms himself. Do not correct a scoffer, lest he hate you; Rebuke a wise man, and he will love you"* (Proverbs 9:7-8).

The person needing to be delivered must first fully humble himself or herself and hate the sins they have been committing. If they say something like, "You know, a lot of us men have this problem," or, "The Lord knows I am weak in this area," – they are not repenting!

If they say, "I have had this problem for a long time," - they are not repenting! It is not a problem. It is wickedness and rebellion against God! If they have been committing sexual immorality and seducing others into sexual sins, they are a fool, and they should repent for being a fool (Psalm 107:17). The New Living Translation translates Proverbs 6:32 to say, *"But the man who commits adultery is an utter fool, for he destroys his own soul."*

Cast Out the Spirits You Have Discerned.

One with a Jezebel spirit must repent of pride, as well as any other vn sins he or she has committed and be willing to have the spirit of pride, as well as the spirit of Jezebel cast out of him. Those with a Jezebel spirit also have what the Bible calls *"a spirit of whoredom"* (Hosea 4:12, 5:4) and *"a perverse spirit"* (Isaiah 19:14, Proverbs 23:29-33). All of this must be repented from and cast out along with the Jezebel spirit.

Notice that the emphasis is on the person with this spirit humbling himself, repenting, and making Jesus Lord. Jesus didn't say He was anointed to pray people through to deliverance.

He said He was anointed to preach deliverance to the captives (Luke 4:18). We do pray for these people and we pray over our part in ministering to them, but we preach to them that they can be free if they choose to be.

Fill up the Void

Before the spirits are cast out, the one being delivered must surrender to the Lordship of Jesus. They should make a firm commitment to read and study the Bible every day (I recommend at least 30 minutes a day) and to pray at least 30 minutes a day.

They must fill the empty place left where the evil spirit was cast out. They must be filled with God's Spirit and His Word so that the spirit will not move back in, accompanied by other evil spirits (Matthew 12:43-45, Luke 11:24-28).

The person being delivered should be willing to be filled with the Holy Spirit and receive a prayer language to help him in his prayer life (I Corinthians 14:2, 13-15).

The Holy Spirit empowers us to live the Christian life. The person should also commit to praying always, with faith, rejoicing in the Lord, and with giving thanks to Him (I Thessalonians 5:16-18). In other words, they must fill their lives with God and His Word.

The good news is that lasting deliverance, freedom, and victory are available through Christ!

If you are an intercession prayer warrior and you want to have maximum effect praying against the Jezebel spirit, knowing the idols that Jezebel worshipped is important.

We are moving into an age where the intercessory body of Christ needs to at least be familiar with these gods and be able to recognize their function when we see them manifest in a person.

Familiarize yourself with the name of the god (idol) and what it was in charge of, then this will become a tool in your belt that you can use in your prayers.

Example:

We are familiar with Mammon. It was a god of riches.

You can find more about Mammon in (Matthew 6:24, Luke 16:9,11,13)

Another is Moloch, the biblical name for a Canaanite god that they sacrificed babies to.

You can find more about Moloch in (Leviticus 18:21,20:2-5, 2 Kings 23:10, Jer 32:35)

Today this is still being done is some demonic cults.

At the back of this book is an Appendix with a list of some of the idols that Jezebel worshipped.

Please do not approach the bully at work and try to cast the Jezebel spirit out of them. That's not where I am going with this.

The Holy Spirit revealed to me that we pray against Jezebel and we have relief for a while but soon we are facing the same problem. We cannot seem to solve the problem completely. It is because we are cleaning out all the little spirits that work for, or alongside Jezebel, but we don't get to the source or the root. (Luke 11:16-36, Matt12:43-45)

When we clean out a house, we need to make sure it is **all** clean. The Spirit reveals something we do in the natural: We leave the window treatments with the house when we move out, and in the spiritual realm, the Jezebel spirit hides behind those curtains. When we are gone, she lets the other spirits back in.

Of course we know not to leave the house empty, but we are not finished cleaning out this house, and with Jezebel still there, satan has a legal right to come back in.

Ok, so here is where you say, "But Marie don't we pray and order Jezebel to get out?" Yes, you do, but Jezebel is **not** her legal name. You need to kick her out using her legal name.

Now I want to speak to you about legal things here for a minute. In the natural world if you have someone renting from you and you need to evict them or if you are buying a house or a car you have to use your legal name, you cannot use a nickname

Jezebel is her nickname!!
Her legal name is Abizebel.

Jezebel is not even her birth name.

Her Phoenician name was **Abizebel,** meaning *"My Father (Baal) is Noble."* The Hebrew scribes deliberately dropped a letter from her name therefore she would be known forever as Jezebel, a dishonorable name meaning, *"Lacking Honor."*

(Brown-Driver-Briggs Hebrew and English Lexicon, Unabridged, Electronic Database. 2002, 2003, 2006 Jezebel Proper name. Also See the Nelson Study Bible, footnote at I Kings 17)

So, when you can pray, use her "legal" name in the eviction and that will take away her legal right to be there.

(This is not the same thing as generational curses. That's a separate thing.)

Remember, when Jesus cursed the fig tree (Matt 11:12-14), he was cursing the root of the tree.

*** *I am NOT saying this is the only way to cast out the Jezebel spirit. I am simply presenting this as an option. You must seek out the Lord as to the direction *specific* to the situation you are dealing with.* ***

If you want to know more about legal rights of the enemy in your life, I would recommend that you search out teachings on the internet. There is some really great information that can be found.

You are going to go into the courts of heaven with this information about Jezebel's legal name. Ask God, the judge, to pass judgment on the enemy and give you a verdict to carry into the battlefield, to decree and declare and execute the verdict of victory over the enemy.

The victory is gained in the courtroom of heaven first, then you go to the battlefield and execute it. We have been taught to go to the battlefield first and go to war with the enemy, fighting him to gain victory. Wrong.

As to the detailed scriptural teachings on courts of heaven, trading floors, benching, legislating, I recommend searching YouTube.

CHAPTER 4:

Additional Characteristics of Jezebel

We saw how Jezebel's four dominant character traits are sexual immorality, witchcraft, hatred of the Word of the Lord, and the way she puts herself forward to be a leader. Here are some other character traits of Jezebel:

1. Jezebel intimidates and seeks to instill fear.

Those who are led by a Jezebel spirit have not crucified their flesh. They have a gift from hell of instilling fear into people, just as Jezebel instilled fear in Elijah and he ran for his life (I Kings 19:1-4). This was right after he had a great victory, killing 850 false prophets! But Jezebel threatens, "I am gonna get you!" and he feared for his life and ran.

From this we can learn: Don't let your guard down right after a big victory, for Jezebel threatens after being threatened.

If Jezebel wanted to kill Elijah, she definitely would have thought of a way to do it. She would have sent an **assassin,** not a messenger (1kings 19:2). She was the queen and was acting in full power as though she was king. Jezebel's message is sent out, by a messenger, to instill fear. She likes to play with her food.

Through this fear, she seeks to control. Be sure not to allow a spirit of fear, coming from a Jezebel, or anywhere else, to chase you out of your church, calling, or ministry. Stay where God wants you. Don't allow a spirit of fear to push you out of your destiny. Fear tempts you to want to give up.

The answer is: Submit to God, and resist the spirit of fear, and he will flee from you (James 4:7). Command him to go from you in the name of Jesus! The Jezebel spirit is not strong, compared to God.

Always Remember:
Jesus' authority trumps Satan's power!

Jesus said, *"Behold, I give you the authority to trample on serpents and scorpions and over all the power of the enemy, and nothing shall by in any means hurt you"* (Luke 10:19). Evil spirits are subject to us through the name of Jesus our Lord (Luke 10:20). Through the name of Jesus, we have authority and power over the spirits behind a Jezebel.

Also ask God to fill you with his love. Remember that perfect love casts out all fear: I John 4:18 NIV: *"There is no fear in love. But perfect love drives out fear, because fear has to do with punishment. The one who fears is not made perfect in love."*

2. Jezebel hates the dignity and sanctity of life and desires to destroy all life that is in the *Image of God.*

Jezebel promoted the worship of Baal, a god of the Canaanites and the Phoenicians. He was a god of war, nature, and fertility. The worship of Baal was mainly concerned with fertility rites and employed many female and male prostitutes. However, at times, the sacrifice of children was included in Baal worship: They *"have filled this place with the blood of the innocents (they have also built the high places of Baal, to burn their sons with fire for burnt offerings to Baal . . . "* (Jeremiah 19:4c-5a, NKJV).

Jezebel, who was very zealous of the worship of Baal, approved of the killing of the innocent babies and small children. The following Scriptures tell us that God is certainly opposed to the killing of babies and children, for He knew us before we were born. You were someone before you were conceived:

Isaiah 44:24 English Standard Version (ESV)

"Thus says the Lord, your Redeemer,

who formed you from the womb:

"I am the Lord, who made all things,

    who alone stretched out the heavens,

    who spread out the earth by myself"

Psalm 71:6 English Standard Version (ESV)

"Upon you I have leaned from before my birth;

    you are he who took me from my mother's womb.

My praise is continually of you."

Jeremiah 1:5 English Standard Version (ESV):

"Before I formed you in the womb I knew you,

and before you were born I consecrated you;

I appointed you a prophet to the nations."

Galatians 1:15 English Standard Version (ESV):

"But when he who had set me apart before I was born, and who called me by his grace . . ."

3. Jezebel does not operate under God's authority, but operates under an illegitimate and usurped authority.

Naboth, a common landowner who lived close to King Ahab's palace in Jezreel, was asked to give his land to Ahab in exchange for some compensation. Naboth owned a vineyard that bordered the palace of the king. Ahab said to Naboth, *"Give me your vineyard so I can use it as a kitchen garden; it's right next to my house – so convenient. In exchange I'll give you a far better vineyard, or if you'd prefer, I'll pay you money for it"* (I Kings 21:2, The Message).

Naboth would not agree to the deal because the land was his inheritance that had been passed down by his ancestors. He told Ahab, *"I will never turn over my family inheritance to you"* (I Kings 21:3a, The Message). Ahab went home angry and discouraged, and he went to bed with his face to the wall refusing to eat.

When Jezebel found Ahab in this mood, she asked him what the matter was. He replied, "I asked Naboth to sell me his vineyard or to trade it, and he refused!" (I Kings 21:6, NLT)

Jezebel sees an opportunity here to take control. She says to Ahab, "Are you not the king? Get up and have dinner and enjoy yourself."

Then Jezebel wrote a letter in Ahab's name and sealed it with the king's seal. The letter called for a meeting of the men of Jezreel. It said to the effect: "Make sure Naboth is there and prepare two worthless men who will swear that they heard Naboth speak words of cursing against God and against the king. Then take Naboth out and stone him to death." The men followed Jezebel's orders and Naboth was dragged outside the city and stoned to death.

When Jezebel got word that the deed was completed, she said to Ahab, "Now you can take the vineyard you wanted, for Naboth is dead." So Ahab went down to claim the vineyard as his own.

Jezebel had no authority to do the things she did. She took liberties and Ahab didn't do anything about it. In the same way, if you run into a Jezebel, he or she will operate under an illegitimate and usurped authority.

The leaders of the church of Thyatira should have stopped the false prophetess, Jezebel, from teaching in the church, but instead they allowed it. King Ahab should have stopped Jezebel from writing a letter in his name, but he allowed it. One with a Jezebel spirit bucks God's authority and brazenly trespasses into forbidden areas.

A Jezebel-type person will start a Bible study without asking the leadership of the church. When asked about it, he or she will turn it around and say something like, "What? The church doesn't want us to have a Bible study? How can the church not want us to read our Bibles?" This is sometimes followed by a split in loyalties between the Jezebel and the leadership of the church.

A Jezebel goes to a local church, but doesn't like authority unless she is in the position of authority. And she will volunteer all right, but in order to establish control.

She seemingly has endless energy and eagerly looks for opportunities to be in charge of projects. Although she will work hard, her motive is never pure, and eventually her secret agenda cannot be hidden.

4. She is pushy, domineering and controlling.

When Jezebel saw something and she didn't like the way it was going, she would use whatever violence necessary to dominate the situation and have her way. We see this in the way she tried to kill all the Lord's prophets and how she had Naboth killed.

She was going to teach Ahab her philosophy to success in life: "Take what it is that you want and destroy anyone who stands in your way." Ahab did not have the courage to stop her.

A person with a Jezebel spirit pressures others to do things, subtly ripping from them their right to choose or make decisions for themselves. She makes others feel as though they don't have enough sense to think for themselves.

In order to dominate, Jezebel must persuade others that she is always right. She is usually quick to express her opinion in any area and she leaves little room for anyone to point out the other side of an issue.

She doesn't want to be questioned. She portrays those who question her as rebels. You need to ask yourself, though, "How can one person be right every time?"

5. She uses manipulation.

Also, in this account about Naboth, we witness how Jezebel manipulated events with her lies and the shameful letter she wrote. She was a master of manipulation.

In order to manipulate, a Jezebel will sometimes use flattery. She will flatter you and try to get on your good side, but it is all manipulation. She always has an agenda. Every move she makes is calculated, and it is a means to an end.

She is so full of deceit that she becomes more and more deceived herself. The book of Jude warns of deceivers who flatter people in order to gain advantages with them and over them (Jude 16).

Jezebel uses her manipulation on those who are in authority. She will not take the side of the employer or a person in authority, unless it is a temporary action to make herself look good. Her main desire is for power, control, and recognition.

Sometimes a Jezebel will use gift-giving as a form of manipulation. She might give a gift to make you feel obligated to her or to make sure you don't confront her with the truth. Naturally, not everyone who gives gifts is guilty of control, but gift-giving is a tactic sometimes used by those who manipulate.

6. She hides the truth.

In the story of Naboth we also see Jezebel hiding the truth and coming up with a fabricated story to replace it. She didn't tell the men of Jezreel the true story – that Ahab asked Naboth to sell his property to him and Naboth refused. She hid that and made up a whole different narrative.

7. She is a convincing liar.

A Jezebel lies convincingly. No one can lie better than she. Jezebel's letter about Naboth was full of lies. She can turn on the charm and make you believe blue is red. She fools those whom she's just met while those who have been victimized by her tactics stand by helplessly. The fact that Jezebel can look you in the eye and lie shows how strong and adamant this deceiving and rebellious spirit is.

8. She is very critical.

We know Jezebel was well-practiced at criticism when we see how she criticized General Jehu. As he approached her palace, she said to him from the upper story window, *"Have you come in peace, you murderer? You are just like Zimri, who murdered his master!"* (I Kings 9:31).

Zimri was a military commander who shamefully killed Israel's King Elah and all his royal family, just so he could make himself king. He only reigned for seven days, though, until the people demanded that he be replaced (I Kings 16:8-11, 15-16).

Jezebel insinuated that a similar thing would happen to Jehu, but that was not the case. Jehu reigned over Israel for 28 years.

Today's Jezebels are also critical. If someone else has a good suggestion, plan, or idea, a Jezebel will look for a way to criticize it, often sharply and quickly, because the idea did not originate from her. Criticizing others elevates the controller in her own mind.

Pastors or evangelists who are dominated by a Jezebel spirit love to criticize others in ministry. They love show off "their special insight that the spirit gave them" about other ministers – how those ministers are falling short.

Each time they criticize another big, well-known ministry and craftily put those ministries down, they are trying to exalt themselves and their own ministry higher.

They like to be the center of attention and when someone else is recognized, they are prone to quickly say things to undermine the person's accomplishments.

Also, "ministers" with a Jezebel spirit stir up strife between themselves and good ministers. They seem to always be in conflict, friction, disagreement, dissension, dispute, or controversy!

As a Jezebel goes about criticizing others in order to exalt herself, she likes to share little secret tidbits with people about other people. Many of these things are told in confidence.

Jezebel tries to make you feel compelled to tell her secret things. She will ask a question to get you to talk and talk, then she will ask another question. After she gathers secret information, she has a sense of power from this knowledge. And she will use this knowledge to put others down and exalt herself.

A Jezebel will continually belittle another person in the most creative and subtle ways. The strategy is to gain control by minimizing the value of another person.

It is common for her to tell half-truths to implicate another person in your eyes. By sowing these seeds, she hopes to push down the person she is criticizing and to improve her position of power.

9. Jezebel uses the element of surprise.

Jezebel's attack on Naboth was a quick, surprise attack. One day Naboth was considered to be an upright, honest and good citizen. Then suddenly Jezebel set him up and falsely accused him so that he would be viewed as a criminal who deserved death.

It was all done so quickly! False evidence, false testimony, then a quick trial which was immediately followed by an execution (I Kings 21:7-13).

Jezebel's main concern is to be in control, and a large part of control is catching people off guard. Therefore, the element of surprise works well when she shows up unexpected, a day early for a meeting, at your home or some other place.

10. Jezebel gathers information to use against you.

Just as Jezebel gathered enough information to overthrow Naboth, today's Jezebels gather information to use against people. Jezebel loves to be in control of information. If there is ever a situation where information is important, she will push to be the first to know it. She seems to know everything about everyone. She has instant recall of data and details about people's lives, especially data she can use against them. Having information which others do not have is a powerful weapon of control for her. Jezebel uses the Delilah spirit to gather information. (Judges 16) shows an example of Delilah at work gathering information to use against Samson.

As she tells her secret facts about people, with intimidation, she seems to be saying, "I know these things about this person and if you were as spiritual and mature as I am, you would know them too."

I worked for a lady that was the manager of operations over a whole department. She told me right from the start that she wanted me to have the position that someone else currently had.

She would then confide in me information regarding employees that worked for her indicating that she did not trust them, but she trusted me.

I was careful to not tell her anything about me, knowing the information she gathered about me would be told to them. Any information I gave her would be sharpened into bullet that later would be fired at me with an aim to kill.

11. Jezebel is vengeful.

As soon as Jezebel found out that Elijah executed all 450 prophets of Baal and all 400 prophets of Asherah, her first thought was vengeance! (I Kings 19:1-2). She then, *"immediately sent a messenger to Elijah with her threat: 'The gods will get you for this and I'll get even with you! By this time tomorrow you'll be as dead as any one of those prophets'"* (I Kings 19:2, *The Message*).

Jezebel considers those who contradict or confront her as enemies. As long as you are in agreement with her, all is well. But if you confront or challenge her, then look out. She will at least speak things to try to intimidate you or destroy your reputation.

I once worked in the northern part of Alberta, Canada, close to the Northwest Territories. I was there for all of November and December. Shortly after I arrived at my location, the boss and I disagreed about some important details and he ceased all communication with me. I was frozen out.

He scheduled me to manage the graveyard shift, so I would never have any contact with him or the others with whom I was supposed to work. I had to negotiate a room in a small local motel so I could walk to work. At the end of a few months when it was time for me to return home, he mentioned to me that had I cooperated more with him, I would have been eligible for a big bonus. I seriously doubt it.

A Jezebel may even speak some judgment prophecies or curses against someone in order, "to clean up the state of the Church". A few years ago, a man walked up in a large meeting, publicly confronted the minister and told him he was false. This "prophet" then prayed, "Kill him, Jesus!"

Another "prophet" was scheduled to speak at a large Christian meeting, but before the day of the meeting some leaders in the church realized that the man had several of the traits which I am discussing in this book.

As soon as the meeting started, two leaders ushered him out of the building. As they did so, this "prophet" began to curse the leader who was throwing him out, and say to him, "Because of this, you are going to become a very broken man."

12. She is independent and closed to correction.

The Biblical Jezebel never received correction from anyone. She kept herself independent and separate from those who might have corrective input to speak to her. A Jezebel won't listen to anyone unless they are cooperating with her agenda. There are those in ministry who are like this; they isolate themselves from anyone who would speak correction into their lives.

13. She is proud and haughty.

Jezebel has a proud spirit. This is obvious from the description of her in the Bible, and from much of what we have already seen in her other traits. A Jezebel is not interested in real, sincere prayer to our true and living God, because then she would have to really humble herself and repent of her wicked ways.

If she gets caught in wrongdoing, she is not sorry for what she did, but rather only sorry that she got caught. She might pray, trying to manipulate God, so that she can gain the favor and honor she had before she was exposed in her sins. It is possible for a Jezebel to repent, but some receive their last call from God to repent and decide not too.

14. A Jezebel minister becomes more and more isolated from other ministers.

A Jezebel, especially one who is leading a church or other ministry, does not have any close friends except those who follow him or her blindly and don't question anything.

I knew a pastor who, when his ministry was good, had visiting ministers come through his church, one about every three to six months. They were also his friends. By the next year, he started changing into a Jezebel and the church stopped having any more visiting ministers.

Another thing to watch for are those who, overall have a good ministry, but have a few of the traits of a Jezebel. Then they start secretly going into rebellion and idolatry until they become a Jezebel.

s this starts to happen, it is difficult to tell who they are, because they are in change-mode. It is an evil transformation and it is puzzling to those who don't know what is going on and who continue to see these leaders as they were when they were following God.

I recommend that you look up the Scriptures about Jezebel in several translations of the Bible. One of my favorite websites to look up Scripture on is biblehub.com It gives you a nice clean list where you can read the Scripture translated into twenty-five different versions by simply scrolling down.

Scriptures that mention Jezebel: I Kings 16 (all, but especially read verse 31), I Kings 18:4, 13, 19, I Kings 19: 1, 2, I Kings 21: 5, 7, 11, 14, 15, II Kings 9: 7, 10, 20, 30, 36, 37, and Revelation 2:20.)

CHAPTER 5:

Jezebel is no Respecter of Gender

The spirit of Jezebel can operate in a woman or a man. When she operates in woman, that is Satan's answer to a male-dominated world. Jezebel provides false protection to a woman who seemingly was never granted her rights or never had the protected love of a father or a husband.

Out of the lack of love, the woman rebels against the whole "unloving system" and becomes just like it. The controlled become the controller and the oppressed become the oppressor.

If allowed to, the spirit of Jezebel will influence a woman to misuse and twist her three God-given gifts: intuitiveness, sensitivity, and compassion. Satan gets her to use her position as a woman inappropriately, until she becomes very developed in her ability to manipulate others without the use of physical strength.

The characteristic of being critical, which we described in chapter four, operates when a woman says demeaning things about her husband and cloaks her comments in humor. Some men are afraid of such a wife. They fear her words and get intimidated by her threats.

Jezebel operates in a man when the enemy capitalizes on a man's wounded areas and influences him to be very controlling of his wife and others through fear and intimidation.

There have been instances when a man with a Jezebel spirit was a pastor of a church and consequently, people became vulnerable to all kinds of abuse. Because of the pastor's boldness, strong authority, (false) anointing, and smooth talk, he could get some of his people to believe just about anything.

He could convince people of things which they normally would not go for. This is an ancient dominating spirit in operation. It is not just some skill from the mind or the personality.

I read a story of a pastor who claimed that the Lord spoke to him about a revolutionary way he could grow the church by allowing people to switch partners in marriage. Of course, he needed to lead by example.

He was the first one to switch. The church, which had been a growing and thriving church, became so perverted that once the thrill of sin for a season was over, it closed. Many of the marriages were destroyed and a number of the women were pregnant with other men's children.

This Jezebel of a pastor sold this idea to them by saying that they were getting to a higher place in God, and should be unashamed of this revelation.

Only a seducing spirit, working in the pastor and in the people, could make such ridiculous perversion seem right. Such a spirit has supernatural power to influence and control people who give into it.

Today approximately 52% of all Christian marriages end in divorce. The spirit of Jezebel is one of the spirits the devil is using to break up families and destroy God's plans, purposes, and destinies for believers. However, we don't have to give the spirit of Jezebel any place in our lives. *"Give no place to the devil"* (Ephesians 4:27). If we don't give him any place in our lives or affairs, he doesn't have any place in our lives. But we must stay alert and walk in holiness and not leave any doors open to the devil through disobedience.

Some men under a Jezebel spirit's influence are verbally abusive and have outbursts of temper and rage. Most of them hide things from their wives.

Some will not tell their wives anything about how much money is in the bank or where they are going. If she asks, they will say that it is none of her business. Many of the men with a Jezebel spirit like to dominate because when they were growing up, they never had the control over their lives that they wanted.

CHAPTER 6:

Keeping Free from the Effects of a Jezebel Spirit

I believe at one time or another, all of us have been affected by a Jezebel spirit. When we find ourselves in the midst of the operations of a Jezebel, we must not react improperly, but be ready to react as an overcomer. The following are things we can do to keep ourselves free from the effects of a Jezebel spirit:

1.   Do not become isolated.

When Jezebel vowed to get even with Elijah and have him killed, Elijah ran for his life and isolated himself (I Kings 19:2-4).

We all need time to relax and draw apart and seek God, but don't let your secret place become your hiding place. There is work to be done.

Years ago, a young man was going to church in which the pastor, who at one time was a strong Christian with a good ministry, was secretly turning away from God and becoming a Jezebel.

The young man discerned that something was very wrong about the church, but he could not pin it down. So, he just quit going to any church and isolated himself. This was tragic because not only did he waste years of his life, but also others in the church desperately needed to know about the warnings he was picking up by the Spirit.

If you think you might be affected by a Jezebel, talk with others in the church who are spiritually mature. Each one of us who are hearing God's voice and seeing His dreams and visions know only a part of what the Spirit is saying to our church (I Corinthians 13:12). When we put all the revelations of the body of Christ together, we see much more of the whole picture.

2. Do not give in to discouragement and depression.

Elijah got so discouraged because of Jezebel's threats that he prayed he might die (I Kings 19:4). He felt like no one was standing with him.

When the young man who left that church finally returned to walking in the Spirit with God, he told his friends, "I don't know why I allowed myself to get so discouraged!" There is a lot of confusion and things are hard to understand when a Jezebel is in power.

The devil seeks to get Christians to the place where they are consistently down and depressed. This is a spiritual assault on the mind, trying to get one to open his or her life to an evil thing. If a Christian is already depressed, it makes it easier for the devil to tempt him into other sins. And the enemy looks for a time to come when he will find the person as weak as possible.

Those who are depressed begin to relate to TV commercials about depression. They have thoughts of quitting one thing or another. If they go to a Jezebel, who they think is a wise and anointed minister, Jezebel may counsel them to quit their marriage, even though their spouse loves them and has been faithful to them.

We must stay close to strong Christian friends who can encourage us when we are tempted to be discouraged. We should also encourage ourselves in the Lord by believing and speaking His promises and by getting built up by praying in the Spirit (I Samuel 30:6, KJV).

3. Refuse self-pity.

When we read the description of Elijah telling the Lord how he was the only faithful one left and Jezebel was trying to kill him, too, we detect a note of self-pity in his words (I Kings 19).

Self-pity takes us out of the battle and out of our place of victory. It isolates us and puts us in a perfect spot for Jezebel to attack on another level. Therefore, speak God's promises out loud to yourself and stand in faith on them. Praise and thank God and declare God's Word over yourself

4. Reject temptations to sin.

Those who commit adultery with Jezebel open themselves up to sickness, physical disorders, and a lack of answered prayer (Revelation 2:20-23). Even those who are innocent of that sin can find their blessings really limited because of their close association and affiliation with Jezebel.

It is like the time when Joshua and Israel were defeated because they had an Achan (a rebel and an idolater) in their camp (Joshua 7:1-26). If you find yourself in spiritual fellowship with a Jezebel, separate yourself immediately!

5. Don't receive false guilt.

When Jezebel tried to make general Jehu feel guilty for killing King Joram (something which God had told him to do), Jehu totally disregarded her false evaluation of him (II Kings 9:30-31).

When a Jezebel falsely evaluates us, accuses us, and paints a false picture of us, we must totally reject her lies.

We may not immediately say something to the Jezebel to defend ourselves, but we should listen closely to what the Holy Spirit says to us so we will know what to say and when to say it. We should ask, "What does God's Word say about me?" We know we are not perfect, but we are the righteousness of God through Christ and there is no condemnation for us who are in Christ Jesus and are living for Him (II Corinthians 5:21, Romans 8:1).

It is good to declare, "I am the righteousness of God through Jesus Christ my Lord!" and, "There is no condemnation for me, for I am in Christ Jesus and I walk after the Spirit and not after the flesh."

6. Watch out for of misuse of the Scriptures.

Jezebel will use plenty of Scriptures. I believe the Jezebel in Thyatira *seemed to be* a legitimate teacher because of her knowledge and use of the Scriptures, and her false gifts which looked and sounded like the true gifts of the Spirit.

There was a young man who listened to the teaching of a Jezebel until he realized what he was dealing with. After he disassociated with that teacher, he described to his friend how that teacher had a subtle way of using Scriptures.

Instead of using them to promote Jesus and His gospel, he would put himself in the place of the Lord and use the Scriptures to validate himself. One day he proclaimed, "The Lord told me that in the same city in which they crucified me, God will raise me up!" What really happened was that people rejected him because he was false. But he interpreted their rejection as persecution of his ministry.

A Jezebel will quote, misquote, partially quote, or misapply Scriptures just like the devil did with Jesus in the desert. When the devil dared Jesus to jump off the highest point of the temple, he said, "If you are the Son of God, throw yourself down.

For it is written: *"He will command his angels concerning you, and they will lift you up in their hands, so that you will not strike your foot against a stone"* (Matthew 4:5-6**)**.

The devil quoted these verses out of context and left out the preceding verses: *"If you make the Lord your refuge, if you make the Most High your shelter, no evil will conquer you; no plague will come near your home"* (Psalm 91:9-10).

The devil left out the condition that the promise was based upon. He also left out the following verse in Psalm 91:13, about us treading the serpents under our feet: *"You shall tread upon the lion and the cobra. The young lion and the serpent you will trample underfoot."* I can see why the devil would not want to quote that part.

Use discernment in listening to and following any teaching, but especially with the teacher who has several or all of the bad characteristics which we have been discussing.

7. Avoid pride.

Jezebels have a proud and haughty spirit. This is actually a demon who empowers a Jezebel person and deals in heavy-duty pride. (Proverbs 21:24) If you get "under their ministry," they will caution you not to visit other churches or to listen much to parachurch ministries.

If you obey a Jezebel, she will put you in a spiritual jail where you are in bondage to her and kept apart from other ministries that you really need. This would surely stunt your growth.

Also, a Jezebel likes to infer that she and those who follow her understand the Scriptures in a superior way. A pastor who became a Jezebel announced to his church, "I don't know of anywhere in the world where there is a ministry that is teaching all the good things that we are."

Only those who are spiritually blinded by pride will continue to sit under such a ministry.

8. Watch out for the sheep stealer or a position thief.

A pastor in Texas let a pastor of a church in another city come and minister in his church about three times a year. The visiting pastor had a powerful anointing and an impressive manifestation of spiritual gifts. Most everyone was so excited whenever he came. A few years later, however, the visiting pastor convinced about a third of that congregation to move to his city and be a part of his church.

When the visiting pastor first came, it looked like he just wanted to help. In time, though, he showed that he wanted to take away as many of the first pastor's members as he could.

The visiting pastor started sowing seeds of division when he began to tell his "revelations" about how the first pastor had "gotten off-course." He expressed regret that he was not able to intercede and pray through to save that other pastor from deception.

When people wondered where they could go to church now "that their pastor was deceived," the visiting pastor showed himself as the perfect candidate for the job of being their new pastor.

9. Watch out for any spirit that steers you away from the will and plan of God.

The Jezebel person may consciously realize what he is doing or he may not, but the spirit that is guiding him desires to control your destiny. The spirit behind such a person will manipulate you and lie to you in order to steer you in another direction other than the one the Lord desires for you.

If he can, one led by this spirit will stop you from completing your work for the Lord, which is always work that is against the enemy's kingdom.

10. Separating yourself from one with this spirit.

I share these things because some who have no knowledge of this spirit's personality will not detect her and she will bring damage to their lives. You can be civil towards the person with this spirit, but you cannot be gracious with the spirit or be in fellowship with it.

When you tell a Jezebel that unless he or she repents you don't want to have anything more to do with him or her, many times such a person will complain about everyone rejecting them and start crying or carrying on in a dramatic way, trying to make you feel guilty for "not handling the situation right."

CHAPTER 7:

Multiple Spirits

Jesus said, *"When an impure spirit comes out of a person, it goes through arid places seeking rest and does not find it. Then it says, 'I will return to the house I left.' When it arrives, it finds the house swept clean and put in order. Then it goes and takes seven other spirits more wicked than itself, and they go in and live there. And the final condition of that person is worse than the first"* (Luke 11:24-26, NIV).

We studied this Scripture in chapter three, but here we will look at it from another angle. Jesus summarized this teaching by saying, *"Blessed are those who hear the Word of God and keep it!"* (Luke 11:28).

Here Jesus describes someone who ends up with eight evil spirits in him. How did he get that way? At first, he had one evil spirit and Jesus cast it out of him (Luke 11:14-20). Then the man makes his life look presentable by sweeping up and putting things in order.

But the problem is, he keeps his house empty (Matthew 12:44). He does not fill his heart and life with obedience to the Word of God (Luke 11:28), and with thanksgiving and praise for what God did for him. When the chief spirit finds the man's life empty, there is room for him and seven other evil spirits, whom he welcomes in.

Someone with a Jezebel spirit is influenced by other evil spirits, such as "the spirit of whoredom" (Hosea 4:12, 5:4, II Kings 9:22), a lying spirit (II Kings 22:22), a proud and haughty spirit, which makes the person a scoffer (Proverbs 21:24, 22:10, 9:7-8, 13:1, 14:6, 24:9, 3:34, 29:8, 16:18), a spirit of spiritual slumber (Isaiah 29:10), a thief spirit (Proverbs 24:33-34, John 10:10), an unclean spirit (Mark 5:2, Luke 8:27), and the spirit of bondage (Romans 8:15).

Jezebels usually have most or all of these seven evil spirits, besides the Jezebel spirit. Is there hope for someone like that?

Those with a Jezebel spirit must want to be free and be willing to repent, or else we cannot help them or cast any spirit out of them. They can't love those spirits and cling to them.

They must repent and allow strong believers to cast out the Jezebel spirit as well as other spirits as the Holy Spirit directs. They also must be willing to fill their hearts and lives with obedience to the Word of God.

We who minister to them should study the Scriptures like those I referenced above which tell us the actual names of various evil spirits. Then we depend on Holy Spirit to give us discernment to know exactly which spirits we are dealing with. Then we bind them and cast them out. I recommend the following prayer for discernment, from Philippians 1:9-11, NKJV:

"And this I pray that your love may abound still more and more in knowledge and all discernment, that you may approve the things that are excellent, that you may be sincere and without offense till the day of Christ, being filled with the fruits of righteousness which are by Jesus Christ, unto the glory and the praise of God."

CHAPTER 8:

How to Overcome the Jezebel Spirit

To overcome Jezebel, each of us must first have our house, or our life, in order. If there is any willful and known sin currently in your life, repent, turn from it and surrender and submit to Jesus. Be sure you have a clean slate with God. Be sure you do not have unrepented sins. *"Therefore, submit to God. Resist the devil and he will flee from you"* (James 4:7, NKJV). We could say it this way, "Submit to God. Resist the Jezebel spirit and she will run from you!"

The devil has no authority over you when you are submitted to God. When any believer is submitted to God and resists the devil (whatever evil spirit it is) in Jesus' name, the devil must depart from him (James 4:7).

If you are not yet having victory by yourself, get with strong and wise believers to help you and pray with you. Listen closely to the Holy Spirit. He will lead you in what to do and how to have victory.

If you come across a person who has a Jezebel spirit:

- Pray for that person earnestly and consistently (Ephesians 6:18, 2 Thessalonians 1:11).

- Stay surrendered to God completely yourself and put your trust in Him (Psalm 115:11, 56:11).

- Keep your soul and spirit focused on God and listen for his instructions (Matthew 10:20, Mark 12:30)

- Resist all evil and keep your heart pure and your spirit sweet. (James 4:7)

- Put on the whole armor of God and keep it on (Ephesians 6:10-20).

- Pray Psalm 91 over your life as often as the Lord leads (maybe daily).

- Find at least one strong Christian who has discernment to come alongside you and help you.

- Remember, the battle belongs to the Lord (II Chronicles 20:15, 32:7). Let God do the heavy lifting.

How did Jesus say the leaders at Thyatira were to deal with the Jezebel in their church? He told them not to tolerate her, to not allow her to teach! (or to spread her spiritual poison in the church) Revelation 2:18-23.

A young man felt led by the Spirit to walk seven times around the church building where he attended church. He knew something was wrong in his church, but he didn't know what it was. He had been praying fervently for the church for months.

The entire time he walked around the church, he prayed and confessed, "Jesus Christ is Lord over this church!" This was on a Saturday night. When he got home, he continued his praying and the Lord said to him, "You are strong, and the word of God abides in you. And you have overcome the wicked one" (I John 2:14b). The next morning the pastor was exposed as being a Jezebel, fulfilling all the descriptions I have given in this book. Immediately, all the members of the church, except the pastor's family, left and the church closed.

We must separate ourselves from any Jezebels who refuse to humble themselves and repent. In chapter three, I told about a man who was known to operate powerfully in spiritual gifts being invited to speak at a large Christian meeting.

But not long before the day the meeting was to start, the leaders of the meeting realized this man had several of the Jezebel traits that I have described in this book. The man was called and told that he was no longer invited to speak.

Well, he went to the meeting anyway, believing God to move through him in spiritual gifts, one way or another. He proudly boasted that "his ministry made waves." When one of the leaders saw him, he and a friend ushered the man out of the building.

How did this leadership deal with the Jezebel spirit? They cast the false prophet out of the building! Since then I have heard that this man has been kicked out of several churches. The Apostle Paul instructed, *"Put away from yourselves that evil person"* (I Corinthians 5:13).

We all want to believe the person with a Jezebel spirit will be delivered. However, only through sincere and lasting repentance will the person be delivered. I say lasting repentance because I have seen Jezebels receive deliverance and seem "normal" for a period of time, exhibiting none of their former evil traits.

Later, though, the devil would tempt them to return to their former sins and suddenly and secretly, without warning and before anyone knew it, once again that person was going forth with uncrucified flesh and a new evil anointing. The evil spirit had come back and brought others in with it and that person was worse off than ever.

The good news is that God gives each individual person the freedom of choice. We can help those who really want to be free and to sincerely serve the Lord. We do not, however, tolerate those who insist on yielding to a Jezebel spirit. Instead, we send them out of the church.

We are not fighting for victory . . . but rather we are fighting Jezebel from a place *of* victory:

- *"But thanks be to God, who gives us the victory through our Lord Jesus Christ"* (I Corinthians 15:57, NKJV).

- *"Now thanks be to God who always leads us in triumph in Christ,"* (II Corinthians 2:14, NKJV).

- *"We are more than conquerors through Him who loved us"* (Romans 8:37, NKJV).

Jesus triumphed over Jezebel and all other evil spirits through what He did on the cross:

"Having disarmed principalities and powers, He made a public spectacle of them, triumphing over them in it" (in the cross) (Colossians 2:13-15, NKJV).

Now, Jesus is raised from the dead and is head over all principalities and powers, and we are raised up with Him, *"and you are complete in Him, who is the head of all principality and power"* (Colossians 2:10, NKJV). We are complete in Him who defeated Jezebel and all other demons.

It was through His death on the cross that Jesus destroyed the authority and power of the devil: *"Inasmuch then as the children have partaken of flesh and blood, He Himself likewise shared in the same, that through death He might destroy him who had the power of death, that is, the devil, and release those who through fear of death were all their lifetime subject to bondage"* (Hebrews 2:14-15, NKJV).

Satan has no legal authority over your life except what you have given him: **"He has delivered us from the power of darkness** *and translated us into the kingdom of the Son of His love, in whom we have redemption through His blood, the forgiveness of sins"* (Colossians 1:13-14, NKJV).

We must keep alert and stay in God's Word. *"Be careful - watch out for attacks from Satan, your great enemy. He prowls around like a hungry, roaring lion, looking for some victim to tear apart"* (I Peter 5:8 TLB).

When the devil tempts us or attacks us, we must resist him in faith and make him run from us (I Peter 5:8-9, James 4:7). We must not return to sins we have forsaken, for the devil has authority in darkness (Colossians 1:13). As we walk in the light, the light has authority over darkness.

Don't give a place to the devil. This includes legal rights as well as sin (Ephesians 4:27). Satan (or a Jezebel) has no legal right to act or command against those who are walking in the light.

Praise God, we are overcoming a foe who has already been defeated. And even little children in Christ can overcome these evil spirits: *"Many false prophets have gone out into the world. But . . . you are of God, little children, and have overcome them, because He who is in you is greater than he who is in the world"* (I John 4:1b, 4, NKJV).

APPENDIX:

The gods Jezebel worshipped

Astarte

- 900 BC Phoenicians dedicated their largest temple to Astarte.

- Egyptian goddess of war

- To a lesser extent, goddess of love and fertility.

- Many names in numerous parts of the world.

- She is also known as "Ishtar"

- As "Ishtar," she was all about love. Obsessed with a few men, she insisted she wanted to marry Gilgamesh. He said no, due to sharing stories about the other men she loved and dumped.

Aphrodite

Facts about Aphrodite

- 7th - 8th Century BC

- Aphrodite was the goddess of fertility, love, and beauty.

- Two different stories explain the birth of Aphrodite. The first is simple: She was the child of Zeus and Dione.

- According to the second story, however, Aphrodite rose from the foam of the sea.

- Aphrodite was married to Hephaestus, but Aphrodite did not enter this union of her own volition.

- She and Ares conceived Harmonia, who eventually married Herodotus.

- She was the mother of Hermaphroditus by Hermes.

- Aphrodite and her son Eros (Cupid) teamed up to cause Zeus to fall in love with a human named Europa.

- Aphrodite, Héra, and Athena were the top three contenders for a gold apple marked, "For the Fairest." They asked Zeus to judge the contest, but he refused. Paris, son of the King of Troy, judged the contest instead. Each of the three goddesses promised him something in return and he chose Aphrodite as the winner of the apple. This story of the Judgment of Paris was considered to be the real reason behind the Trojan War.

- During the Trojan War, Aphrodite fought alongside of Paris.

- Aphrodite rescued Paris from Menelaus by enveloping him in a cloud and taking him back to Troy.

- Aphrodite owned a girdle that contained her enchantments; Hera borrowed it once to seduce Zeus in order to distract her from the Trojan War.

- Aphrodite gave Harmonia a necklace that brought disaster to a later generation.

- Prostitutes considered the goddess of love their patron.

- Aphrodite had a few mortal lovers. One of the most notable was the Trojan shepherd Anchises. The two of them conceived Aeneas.

- Corinth was the center of Aphrodite's worship.

- Early Greek art depicted the goddess as nude.

- She was the model for the famous sculpture Venus de Milo.

- Aphrodite and Cupid initiated the love between Jason (hero of the Quest of the Golden Fleece) and the daughter of the Colchian King.

Hathor- Goddess of fertility

- Hathor was also the goddess of beauty and patron of the cosmetic arts. Her traditional votive offering was two mirrors and she was often depicted on mirrors and cosmetic palettes. Yet she was not considered to be vain or shallow, rather she was assured of her own beauty and goodness and loved beautiful and good things.

- She was known as "the mistress of life," and was seen as the embodiment of joy, love, romance, perfume, dance, music and alcohol.

- She was a sky goddess, known as "Lady of Stars" and "Sovereign of Stars," and linked to Sirius (and so the goddesses Sopdet and Isis).

Seth

- God of windstorms, evil chaos and darkness, and confusion.

- Egyptian God

- Wide-eared animal head on a man's body. Sometimes depicted as a hippopotamus, pig or donkey.

- Mainly worshipped in lower Egypt

Asherah

(I Kings 11:5, 11:33, 14:15, 14:23, 15:13, 16:33, 18:19, 2 Kings 17:10, 23:13, 17:16, 13:6, 2:3, 21:3, 21:7, 23:4, 23:4,7 Deuteronomy 16:21, I Samuel 31:10, 7:3, 12:10, Isaiah 27:9, Judges 3:7, 2:13, 10:6 Jeremiah 17:2, 7:18, 44:17-19, 25)

- Goddess of heaven.

- Thought to be the lost bride of Yahweh (this is false)

- Pole-like symbol

- Found in the temple of Solomon

- Women wove hangings dedicated to her, hanging them on the temple wall

- Images were in people's homes.

- Mother goddess of Canaanites

- Wife of whichever male god had the upper hand.

- Referred to as Wisdom and the tree of life.

I have traced these idols all the way back to the Canaanites. Here is a list of them. They can be found online in history records.

Nergal - god of war.

Mot - god of death and sterility.

Resheph - got of the plague and underworld.

El - possessor of heaven & earth.

Zeus - sender of thunder, lightning, rain, wind.

Dyaus - sky god

Athena - goddess of war.

Artemis - goddess of the hunt.

Minerva - worshipped as goddess of war.

Apollo - god of sun, light, music, poetry, healing, plagues, prophecy, knowledge, order, beauty, archery, and agriculture.

Horus - sky god.

Prometheus - gave fire and skill for metal work.

Odin - the one to council with before going to war.

Dionysus - responsible for prosperity in wine, wine-making, grape cultivation. Also, for human fertility.

Mars - god of war

Isis - most important goddess in Egypt. Magical healer of the dead.

Vestal virgin - six priestesses who attended the sacred fire in the shrine of Vestal.

Thoth - judgment of the dead, development of science.

Anna Perenna - goddess of the new year and time

Ares - god of war.

Demeter - goddess of grain and agriculture.

Hephaestus - was the god of fire, metalworking, stone masonry, forges, and art of sculpture.

Hypnos - god associated with sleep. Mother Nyx (night) father Erebus (darkness).

Janus - animistic spirit of doorways and archways.

Nike - means to attack vehemently.

Nemesis - goddess of divine retribution and revenge.

Iris - personification of the rainbow. A messenger of the gods.

Hecate - guardian of the household/ protector of newborns. Goddess of witchcraft.

Fortuna - goddess of chance. Bearer of prosperity and increase.

Myth - god in charge of extraordinary events and circumstances.

Seth, Asherah, Hathor

Astarte

For references here, I read all over the Internet. It is easy to find if you google ancient gods or idols.

Bibliography

Bolger D. & Serenity N., editors. Engendering Aphrodite, Women and Society in Ancient Cyprus. ASOR Archaeological Report 7, Boston, 2002.

Brenner, Athalya & Willem van Henten, Jan, editors. Bible Translation on the Threshold of the Twenty- First Century. London: Sheffield Academic Press Ltd, 2002.

Budin, Stephanie L. "A Reconsideration of the Aphrodite - Ashtart Syncretism". Numen. 51, 2. P. 95–145, 2004.

Byblos, Jem'appelle and Thiollet, Jean-Pierre. H & D, 2005.

Chadjiioannou, K. Ancient Cyprus in Greek sources, B, Nicosia, 1973

Daressy, Georges. Statues de Divinités (CGC 38001-39384), vol. II. Cairo: Imprimerie de l'Institut français d'archéologie orientale, 1905.

Day, John. "Yahweh and the gods and goddesses of Canaan", p.128. Books.google.com.au. 2002-12- 01. Retrieved 2014-04-25.

Griffiths, J. Gwyn, Plutarch's De Iside et Osiride, p. 325–322.

Harden, Donald. The Phoenicians (2nd ed., revised). London: Penguin Books, 1980.

Karageorghis, J. La Grande. Deesse de Chypre et son culte, Lyon, 1977.

Murphy, Charles. BURNING TIMES/CHANT, in Internet Book of Shadows, (Various Authors), [1999], at sacred- texts.com.

Patai, Raphael. The Hebrew Goddess. Wayne State University Press 1990. p. 57.

Powell, Barry B. Classical Myth with new translation of ancient texts by H. M. Howe. New Jersey: Prentice Hall Inc. 1998. p. 368.

Radmacher, Earl D. editor. The Nelson Study Bible. Nashville: Thomas Nelson Inc., 1997.

Russell , Jeffrey Burton. The Devil: Perceptions of Evil from Antiquity to Primitive Christianity. Cornell University Press 1977, p. 94.

Scherm, Gerd. Brigitte Tast, Astarte und Venus. Eine foto- lyrische Annäherung. Schellerten, 1996.

Snaith, The Interpreter's Bible, 1954, Vol. 3, p. 103.

Smith, Mark S. "The early history of God", Books.google.com.au. 2002-08-03. Retrieved 2014-04-25, p.129.

Stone, Merlin. "When God Was A Woman" (Harvest/HBJ, 1976)

Wunderlich, R. The Secret of Creta. Athens: Efstathiadis Group. 1987. p. 134.

Abizebel name found: Brown-Driver-Briggs Hebrew and English Lexicon, Unabridged, Electronic Database. 2002, 2003, 2006 Jezebel Proper name, feminine.

FREE gift of Bonus material about the role that Rejection played in the lives of Ahab and Jezebel.

FREE Bonus

Go to https://mariemoyers.activehosted.com/f/5.

My Website is MarieMoyers.com

Book Website is JezebelExposed.com

Please leave a positive review with Amazon, as an author it is our lifes blood.

For your ease and convenience this is the link to the review page for my book: https://amzn.to/32TqpFB

Made in the USA
San Bernardino, CA
15 November 2019